REMARKABLE LIVES

Stephen HAWKING

Kitty Ferguson

PITKIN

Introduction

In 1988, the photo of a scholarly-looking gentleman in a wheelchair appeared on the cover of a new book, *A Brief History of Time*. No one could have predicted the book's enormous success, or that the face on the cover would soon be familiar worldwide.

Stephen Hawking, whose books and documentaries would lead us into black holes and to the origin of the universe, drew multitudes to his lectures, from Beijing to Cambridge to California. Leaders of governments and science awarded him medals. The media followed him like a rock star. He suffered from a debilitating disease that is usually fatal in two or three years, yet he survived triumphantly to the age of 76. His ashes were interred in Westminster Abbey.

How did an unexceptional schoolboy from St Albans become Lucasian Professor of Mathematics at Cambridge and one of the most inspiring figures of the twentieth and twenty-first centuries? How did he accomplish all he did in spite of the physical destruction of motor neurone disease, able to communicate only by choosing words from a computer screen by moving his cheek?

The story is incredible, but it isn't fiction.

In 1983, Hawking was a familiar and easily recognizable figure in the streets of Cambridge and the College courts, but he was not yet an international celebrity.

Childhood

In January 1942, with wartime bombs falling on London, it seemed wise to Dr Frank Hawking and his wife Isobel, living in Highgate, for her to move to Oxford for the birth of their first child. The son born there on 8 January was christened Stephen William. When the boy was eight, his father became head of the Division of Parasitology at the National Institute for Medical Research, and the family moved to St Albans. By that time Stephen had two younger sisters. He had not yet learned to read.

A curious child

The Hawkings spent the summers of Stephen's childhood in a field at Osmington Mills, on the Dorset coast. They travelled there in an old London black taxi cab with a table added between the back seats for the

The rocky coast of Dorset, where the Hawking family spent summers when Stephen was a child, had once been smuggler territory.

children to play games while they drove. Once arrived, they camped in a ramshackle gypsy caravan and a large tent. In what had once been smuggler territory, the children explored the rocky beach, and Stephen discovered fossils that first awoke in him a sense of wonder for life on Earth.

Far from city lights, the boy watched the stars – something he would love to do all his life. With his sisters he clambered over rocks and raced across fields and beach, with no idea that his days of climbing and running were numbered . . . no hint of the tragedy that lay ahead, or of the courage he would need to face it. Beginning in his early twenties, he would slowly but inexorably lose his ability to move or speak and be left physically helpless, silent and frozen, slumped in a wheelchair. That fragile figure is now familiar to millions as an intellectual giant of our contemporary world – and among the bravest and most inspiring of its men and women.

Stephen later said he was grateful that he had a normal, healthy, active childhood before the onslaught of motor neurone disease in his early twenties.

An Unexceptional Student

Between the boy of the Osmington beach summers and the Cambridge graduate student of the early 1960s, locked in a deteriorating body, there were years of growing up in St Albans and as an undergraduate at Oxford. As a schoolboy Stephen was no prodigy. He bothered to learn only what interested him and what he thought useful, and was ranked in the lower half of his class. 'It was a very bright class', he later claimed. What did interest him was taking things apart to find out how they worked, mathematics, and building a computer with friends and a favourite teacher. Some at St Albans School recognized that within this mediocre little scholar lurked an interesting mind.

Casually inviting disaster

Stephen surprised them all, and his parents, by his sterling performance in entrance exams and interviews for Oxford. However, once there, reading physics as an undergraduate at University College, his slipshod study habits continued. Hawking later calculated he had spent an average of one hour a day studying: about one thousand hours in three years (1959–62) at Oxford.

The chief accomplishments of this casually arrogant, popular young man seemed to be as cox of a college boat, and the occasional show-off remark in a tutorial. In his third year, however, he found himself navigating into deeper waters. He was getting clumsy. He had an unexplained fall down stairs. He was also facing exams that would determine his future.

TRIBUTE TO A TEACHER

Hawking wrote of a teacher at St Albans school: 'His classes were lively and exciting. Everything could be debated. Thanks to Mr Dikran Tahta, I am a professor of mathematics at Cambridge… When each of us thinks about what we can do in life, chances are we can do it because of a teacher.'

Stephen (left) and his friends at St Albans School built a remarkable computer that they called LUCE: Logical Uniselector Computing Engine.

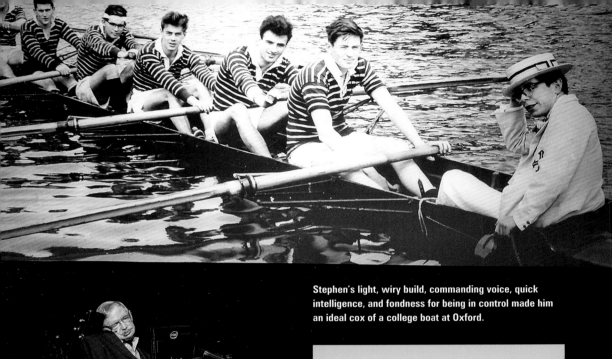

TO WORK OR NOT TO WORK

In Hawking's *A Brief History of Time: A Reader's Companion*, Oxford fellow-student, Gordon Berry, remembers: 'We just didn't apply ourselves. And Steve was right down there in not applying himself.' 'I'm not proud of this lack of work,' Hawking wrote, 'I'm just describing my attitude at the time, which I shared with most of my fellow students: an attitude of complete boredom and feeling that nothing was worth making an effort for. One result of my illness has been to change all that: when you are faced with the possibility of an early death, it makes you realize that life is worth living, and that there are lots of things you want to do.'

Where did the universe come from?

Stephen had decided he wanted to work in theoretical physics, specifically cosmology, feeling (as he told the *New York Times* in January 1983) that '[cosmology] really did seem to involve the big question: Where did the universe come from?'

Cambridge had accepted him for PhD research, conditional on a First Class degree from Oxford. This was no sure thing. His exam results were borderline, and he was summoned for a personal interview or 'viva'. His future in the balance, Stephen produced the kind of off-the-cuff remark well known to his friends: 'If I get a First, I shall go to Cambridge. If I receive a Second, I will remain at Oxford. So I expect that you will give me a First.'

Diagnosis

Hawking's first term at Cambridge was a disaster. Looking forward to working with renowned astronomer Fred Hoyle, he was instead assigned Dennis Sciama as supervisor. Also, Stephen's mathematics background was inadequate for his chosen subject. Yet Sciama proved a fine mentor, less often absent from Cambridge than the world-famous Hoyle. Stephen picked up the mathematics by teaching other students, keeping a few steps ahead. He also travelled regularly to King's College, London, where the physicist Hermann Bondi was lecturing on Einstein's theory of general relativity.

The third problem was the killer – literally. Stephen's clumsiness worsened and he began having problems tying his shoes. His speech became slurred. At home for Christmas, these problems were too obvious to conceal. Frank Hawking took his son to the family doctor, who referred them to a London specialist early in the new year.

Hermann Bondi's lectures on Einstein's relativity theories frequently drew Hawking to London during his first term at Cambridge.

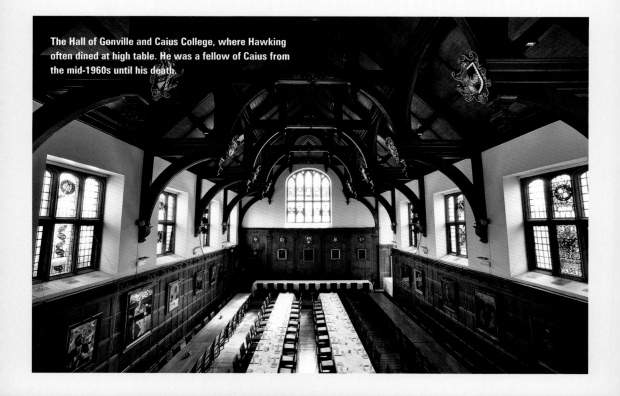

The Hall of Gonville and Caius College, where Hawking often dined at high table. He was a fellow of Caius from the mid-1960s until his death.

NO KNOWN CURE

Hawking had Amyotrophic Lateral Sclerosis (ALS), also known as motor neurone disease, or Lou Gehrig's disease. There is no known cure. Nerve cells in the spinal cord and brain gradually disintegrate, initially causing weakness and twitching of the hands, with perhaps slurred speech and difficulty in swallowing. As nerve cells continue to disintegrate, the voluntary muscles they control atrophy. Eventually movement, speech and normal communication become impossible. Stephen Hawking is not alone in surviving for decades, but death usually occurs within two or three years, from pneumonia or suffocation. ALS does not affect involuntary muscles of the heart, muscles of waste elimination or the sexual organs. The brain remains lucid to the end.

In her 2000 book *Music to Move the Stars: A Life with Stephen Hawking*, Jane Hawking described the Stephen she first met – 'slight of frame, leaning against the wall in a corner, gesticulating with long thin fingers as he spoke – his hair falling across his face over his glasses – and wearing a dusty black-velvet jacket and a red-velvet bow tie.'

Coming of age

That January, 1963, at a New Year's party, Stephen met Jane Wilde, who was soon to leave school to study languages at Westfield College, London University. In her memoir *Music to Move the Stars*, Jane remembered him seeming terribly intelligent, eccentric and rather arrogant, but interesting and she liked his self-deprecating wit. Stephen invited Jane to his twenty-first birthday party, her first experience of his eccentric family. She spent most of the evening near the fire, holding Stephen's young brother Edward on her lap, trying to stay warm in the icy cold house (Frank Hawking was frugal about heating and

repairing broken windows). Stephen's physical problems were growing more severe. He had difficulty pouring drinks.

Stephen spent the weeks following that party in St Bartholomew's Hospital in London. The diagnosis was vague: not a 'typical case' and not multiple sclerosis. He was told to return to Cambridge and continue his work. 'I gathered,' he wrote later (in a private memoir that he later published) 'that they expected it to continue to get worse, and that there was nothing they could do, except give me vitamins. I didn't feel like asking for more details, because they were obviously bad.'

Facing the Future

At 21, Stephen faced a heartbreaking prospect. With typical understatement, he described his reaction in his memoir: 'The realization that I had an incurable disease, that was likely to kill me in a few years, was a bit of a shock. How could something like this happen to me? However, while I had been in hospital, I had seen a boy I vaguely knew die of leukaemia in the bed opposite me. It had not been a pretty sight. Whenever I feel inclined to be sorry for myself, I remember that boy.'

Nevertheless, he became deeply depressed. His doctors could not tell him how quickly he would get worse, or what it would be like. The advice to return to working on his PhD seemed a cruel joke. What point was there in labouring towards a doctorate he would not live to receive? Surely, he thought, they just hoped to keep his mind off the fact that he was dying. He hid away in his Cambridge rooms, listened to the music of Richard Wagner, and occasionally went into the garden to practice croquet shots. But all was not despair. He began seeing Jane Wilde whenever possible.

Defying dire predictions about Stephen's future, he and Jane Wilde married in Cambridge in July 1965.

Felicity Jones and Eddie Redmayne played the roles of Jane and Stephen in the film *The Theory of Everything*, based on Jane Hawking's book *Travelling to Infinity: My Life with Stephen*.

Carrying on

Hawking's condition worsened rapidly but then stabilized. He was buoyed up by his relationship with Jane and a new friend, fellow student lodger Robert Donovan. Dennis Sciama suggested he go back to working on his dissertation, and that was what he did. One encouraging thought was that most work in theoretical physics would take place in his mind. No matter what illness did to his body, it could never touch his intellect.

Stephen Hawking later took issue with the description of him as an extremely courageous man. 'What choice did I have?', he asked. 'One has to be grown-up enough to realize that life is not fair. You just have to do the best you can in the situation you are in. There is always something you can do!' With that attitude, Hawking got on with life and, unbelievable as it seems, somehow managed to treat devastating disability as hardly more than an annoyance. In autumn 1964, Stephen asked Jane to marry him. She agreed.

A big enough question

Stephen Hawking would be renowned not only for his work in theoretical physics, but also for changing his mind, doing abrupt about-faces, and ruthlessly pulling the rug from under his own discoveries and firm assertions. The first 'firm assertion' came early.

Looking for a dissertation subject, Stephen encountered the work of Roger Penrose, at Oxford, who was studying what happens when a star has no nuclear fuel left to burn and collapses under the force of its own gravity. Penrose, building on earlier work by physicists such as Subrahmanyan Chandrasekhar and John Archibald Wheeler, concluded that the star would be crushed to a point of infinite density and infinite curvature of spacetime, a 'singularity' in the centre of what Wheeler was calling a 'black hole'.

A Great, Enormous Big Nothing?

The study of black holes was in its infancy at this time. We now know that there are many in the universe, but not until 2017 were scientists able to photograph one. Black holes are a remarkable phenomenon in science because they were 'discovered' by calculation and theory long before there was even *indirect* evidence.

The birth of a black hole

A star burns for billions of years while a tug-of-war goes on between outward pressures (from nuclear reactions inside the star) and the inward pull of its gravity. When a star runs out of nuclear fuel, gravity wins. The star shrinks, squeezed to greater and greater density. On the star's surface the pull of gravity (or the 'curvature of spacetime', as Einstein preferred) grows increasingly severe. Light from the star finds it difficult to avoid following a path that curves back in.

Last escape

There is a split second when the 'escape velocity' from the star's surface (the speed needed to escape) is not quite the speed of light, but very near. Light can still escape. The curvature of spacetime at the star's surface is *almost but not quite* severe enough to bend the paths of photons (particles of light) coming from the star all the way back in. The last photons that will ever escape do so in this split second. A split second later, the star's surface has shrunk a little further. Escape velocity from the surface is now greater than the speed of light. Nothing can exceed the speed of light. Spacetime curvature at the surface is so great that paths of photons coming from the star are bent back in. The star officially becomes a black hole between the instant-of-last-escape and the instant-of-having-to-be-pulled-back-in.

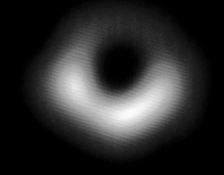

Using data from eight telescopes, worldwide, astronomers produced the first view of a real black hole and released it in March 2019. It is an enormous black hole at the centre of the M87 galaxy, 53 million light years away and 6 billion times larger than our Sun.

A rotating black hole pulls material from a neighbouring star into an 'accretion disk' where it becomes increasingly hot as it spirals nearer to the event horizon. Jets like the one shown here are blasts of material originating outside the event horizon.

Invisible

Imagine an invisible 'surface' at that circumference, the 'boundary' of the black hole, dubbed the 'event horizon'. Some photons stay trapped at that circumference as the star continues to shrink. They will not escape or be pulled back in. Think of them as swarming in a thin, spherical shell surrounding the interior of the black hole. Inside this shell, the star goes on shrinking. Nothing inside this shell can escape . . . or so everyone thought in the early 1970s.

Singularity

Inside the event horizon, the star shrinks until it is compressed to a 'singularity', a point of infinite density and spacetime curvature. Hawking and Penrose defined a black hole as an area of the universe, or a 'set of events', from which nothing can escape to a distance. With its event horizon for an outer boundary, a black hole is shaped like a sphere or, if it is rotating, a bulged-out sphere that would appear elliptical when seen from the side (except you can't see it!).

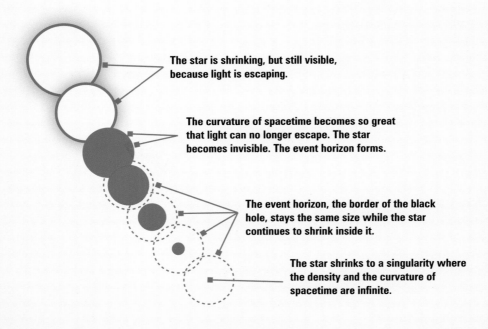

The star is shrinking, but still visible, because light is escaping.

The curvature of spacetime becomes so great that light can no longer escape. The star becomes invisible. The event horizon forms.

The event horizon, the border of the black hole, stays the same size while the star continues to shrink inside it.

The star shrinks to a singularity where the density and the curvature of spacetime are infinite.

Seeking the Origin of the Universe

Hawking decided to investigate whether Penrose's ideas about a star collapsing to a singularity might, with time reversed, apply to the early universe. Suppose all of spacetime -- everything that would later be the universe we know and much we do not -- was once curled up in a dimensionless point, a point of infinite density. Suppose this singularity exploded outwards and expanded. Hawking completed his dissertation in 1965. 'There is a singularity in our past!' he proclaimed.

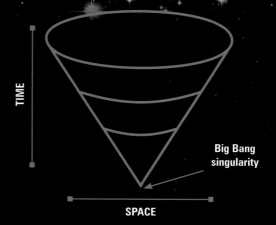

TIME

SPACE

Big Bang singularity

Eddie Redmayne as Hawking in the film *The Theory of Everything*. Delivering a physics lecture requires not only speaking but also writing very lengthy strings of equations on the chalkboard. This became impossible for Hawking by the mid-1960s.

'The toughest man'

Stephen stayed in Cambridge after his PhD, as a research fellow at Gonville and Caius College. His career in theoretical physics moved from strength to strength, and in 1966 he and Roger Penrose were awarded the prestigious Adams Prize by the University of Cambridge Mathematics Faculty and St John's College.

Stephen and Jane's first child, Robert, was born in May 1967. Hawking could still navigate around his home and the Department of Applied Mathematics and Theoretical Physics (DAMTP) with a cane, supporting himself against the wall. Colleagues recall his brashness in sessions where he raised unexpected, penetrating questions, challenging some of the world's most distinguished scientists. His unusual confidence and intelligence, together with his physical problems, distanced him from some in the department but others found him great fun – a gentle, witty, self-deprecating man who was (as the American physicist Kip Thorne described him in a eulogy 50 years later) 'the toughest man I have ever known'.

In the late 1960s, Hawking resorted to crutches, then found it difficult to move

Hawking's smile is radiant in this early snapshot of him with his baby Robert. Four years after doctors had given him two years to live, he was a father.

around even with their aid. It could take him fifteen minutes to climb upstairs to bed, determined to do so without help. His refusal to make concessions to his illness caused difficulties for Jane. But to him, it seemed any concession was an admission of defeat, to be resisted as long as possible. Harder to deal with was the deterioration of his speech. He could no longer give regular lectures. Yet his growing importance as a physicist made him too valuable for his college and university to lose. Gonville and Caius created a six-year fellowship for him in 1969, as Fellow for Distinction in Science.

Laws and Disorder

The Hawking's second child, Lucy, was born in November 1970. Shortly afterwards, an idea occurred to him that he immediately realized had major importance: a black hole can never get smaller because the area of its event horizon, its outer border, can never decrease (see pp. 10–11).

A black hole's size depends on its mass – that is, how much matter is in it. A black hole *can* get larger. It gets larger when anything new falls in past the event horizon and adds to its mass. It would, likewise, get smaller if anything escaped, but nothing can: the escape velocity at the event horizon is the speed of light, and nothing can exceed that speed. A black hole could not possibly lose any mass, so it could not get smaller.

WHAT IS ENTROPY?

An assembled jigsaw puzzle carefully put away in a box might be jostled, mixing up the pieces. More jostling is highly unlikely to make the mixed-up pieces fall back into place and restore the picture. Broken plates never repair themselves. A messy room never tidies itself. 'Disorder' never decreases. 'Entropy' is the amount of disorder in a system – a puzzle box, a room, or the universe.

The *second law of thermodynamics* says that disorder always grows greater, never decreases. If someone reassembles the puzzle, glues the plate or tidies the room, does entropy decrease? No. The mental and physical energy burned in the process converts energy to a less useful form. That means an increase in the amount of disorder in the universe, outbalancing any increase of order achieved by the glueing or tidying.

A new law

Hawking's discovery, known as the *second law of black hole dynamics,* states precisely that: the area of the event horizon can stay the same or increase, but never decrease. Not only can a black hole never get smaller, it cannot be destroyed or divided. If two black holes collide and form one, the area of the new event horizon is as big as, or bigger than, the previous event horizons added together. The first observations of gravitational waves, in September 2015 (see p. 31), have allowed us to begin to test whether this last assertion is correct.

Disorder always gets worse

Hawking and his colleagues noticed that his 'second law of black hole dynamics' resembled another 'second law' in physics: the *second law of thermodynamics*, which has it that entropy, the amount of disorder in a system, can increase but not decrease. Was the resemblance between the two 'second laws' significant?

Hawking watches as Jane Hawking and their two children Robert and Lucy play cricket in their garden in Pasadena California in 1975, during a year-long visit at California Institute of Technology.

Hawking Radiation

Hawking announced in December 1970 his conclusion that the area of the event horizon of a black hole can never get smaller. He conceded that the two 'second laws' are similar, but insisted this was only an analogy, not a true link. Jacob Bekenstein, a graduate student at Princeton, disagreed. The area of the event horizon of a black hole is not only *like* entropy, he insisted, it *is* entropy. When you measure the area of the event horizon, you are measuring the entropy of the black hole.

Thinking big and small

Bekenstein's argument introduced a sticky problem. Physicists know that if something has entropy, it is not totally cold. It has a temperature and it radiates energy. Nothing was supposed to come out of a black hole, but if a black hole radiates energy, then something is coming out. Is that possible? Hawking firmly resisted the idea, but he decided that if anyone

was going to show he was wrong, it had to be himself.

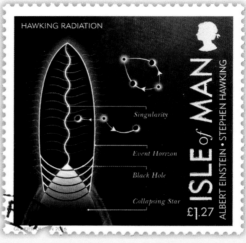

One of six postage stamps, issued in 2016 to celebrate the work of Einstein and Hawking, illustrates the activity of particle pairs at an event horizon in Hawking radiation (see pp. 18–19).

Werner Heisenberg, famous for his 'uncertainty principle', a frustrating feature of quantum mechanics (theories having to do with the activities of the very small: atoms, molecules, and elementary particles).

THE HEISENBERG UNCERTAINTY PRINCIPLE
AND NOT-SO-EMPTY SPACE

There is a frustrating principle in quantum mechanics known as the 'uncertainty principle': it is impossible to know both the position (where it is) and the momentum (how it is moving) of a particle at the same time with complete accuracy. The more precisely its position is measured, the less certain its momentum becomes, and vice versa. This is not a problem caused by lack of skill in measuring. When a particle has an exact position, it does not *have* an exact momentum, and vice versa.

More relevant to Hawking's discovery of Hawking raditiation: The 'uncertainty principle' also holds when we try to measure the value of a field (such as a gravitational field or an electromagnetic field). It is impossible to determine at the same time both the value of a field and the rate at which the field is changing over time. The more precisely the value of a field is known, the less precisely the rate of change is known, and vice versa. In completely empty space – no light or gravity or any other sort of field – it's obvious that with absolutely nothing there, the value of all fields *would* measure exactly zero – a very precise measurement. The uncertainty principle does not allow that. But we don't have completely empty space. There is always at least a minimum amount of uncertainty, or 'fuzziness' as to just what is the value of a field. This uncertainty or fuzziness can be pictured by thinking of pairs of particles (photons or gravitons, for instance) appearing and then, after an interval of time too short to imagine, disappearing. They may not be 'real' particles detectable with a particle detector, but they are not imaginary. We can measure the effects of these 'virtual' particles by their effects on other particles.

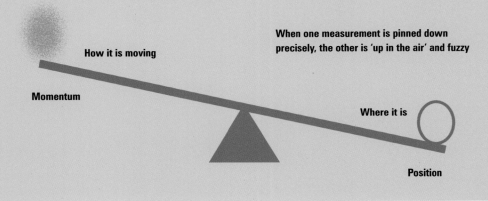

How it is moving

Momentum

When one measurement is pinned down precisely, the other is 'up in the air' and fuzzy

Where it is

Position

Drama at the Event Horizon

The background for Hawking's work on this
problem was the theory that at all times and
everywhere, in what most of us incorrectly
think of as empty space, pairs of virtual
particles – such as photons (particles of light)
and gravitons (particles of gravity) – are
continually appearing and disappearing. Some
pairs are *matter particles*. In this case, one of
the pair is an *antiparticle*. 'Antimatter', familiar
from fantasy games and science fiction (it
drove the starship *Enterprise* in *Star Trek*), is
not purely fictional. The two particles in a pair
separate, then after an interval of time too
short to imagine they meet again and
annihilate one another. Hawking reasoned that
there will be many such pairs popping up near
the event horizon of a black hole. One
member of the pair will have positive energy,
the other negative energy. Before a pair of
these virtual particles meet again and
annihilate, the one with negative energy might
cross the event horizon into the black hole.
The gravitational field at the event horizon is
strong enough to change 'virtual' particles to

View of Earth from the Moon. If the mass of
either the Earth or the Moon changed, the
strength of the gravitational pull between
them would change.

A model of the *Enterprise*
used in the original *Star
Trek of* 1966–69.

'real' particles, and this transformation makes a remarkable difference to the pair. No longer doomed to find one another and annihilate, they can both live longer, and separately. The particle with positive energy might fall into the black hole too, but does not have to. It can escape. To an observer at a distance it appears to come out of the black hole. In fact, it comes from just outside. It is very significant, however, that its partner has carried negative energy into the black hole. The result would come to be known as 'Hawking radiation'.

Negative energy, less mass

Thanks to Albert Einstein, we know that there is an 'equivalence' between energy and mass: if anything loses energy, as a black hole does when a negative particle falls in, it loses mass. As Isaac Newton had discovered, any change in the mass of a body changes the strength of its gravitational pull on another body. If the Earth were to become less massive, its gravitational pull out where the Moon is would become weaker. Likewise, if a black hole becomes less massive, its gravitational pull becomes weaker where the event horizon has been. Escape velocity there becomes less than the speed of light. A new event horizon forms closer in. The black hole has lost mass and become smaller, even though nothing has actually escaped past the event horizon. With this brilliant bit of sleight-of-hand, Hawking began a new era in our thinking about black holes. Hawking radiation is considered his most significant contribution to physics.

THE EQUIVALENCE OF ENERGY AND MASS

Negative means 'minus' (less). When a particle with negative energy carries negative energy into the black hole, that means less energy in the black hole. If a black hole has less energy, it has less mass. In Albert Einstein's equation $E = mc^2$, E stands for energy, m for mass, c for the speed of light. When the energy grows less (as it has in the black hole), something on the other side of the equal sign grows less too. The speed of light (c) cannot change. It must be the mass that grows less. So, when we say a black hole loses energy, we are also saying it loses mass.

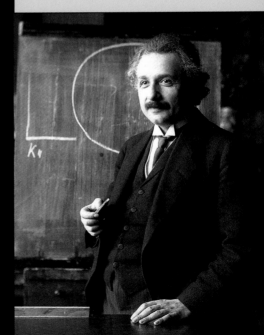

Changing Everything

With Hawking radiation, Hawking showed that his first discovery about black holes (that the area of the event horizon can never decrease) does not always hold – a black hole can get smaller and eventually evaporate entirely. This was the reverse of everything he and all his colleagues had been thinking. He himself had serious doubts about his discovery. It was fearful to predict what others would make of it. If he was right, his findings would revolutionize astrophysics. If he was wrong, he would be ridiculed. He recalculated many times, coming at the problem from one direction after another, never quite satisfied.

Hawking broached the idea to close friends. Martin Rees (later Astronomer Royal) approached Dennis Sciama, exclaiming 'Have you heard? Stephen's changed everything!' Sciama urged Hawking to release his findings. Roger Penrose was enthusiastic. Hawking finally agreed to announce his discovery, but he hedged his bets by putting a question mark after his title: 'Black Hole Explosions?'

'Absolute rubbish'

The presentation in February 1974, at the Rutherford Appleton Laboratory near Oxford was short, greeted with silence and few questions. Many listening were experts in other fields and Hawking's arguments went over their heads. It was obvious to those who did understand that his proposition ran contrary to accepted theory, but to raise a meaningful argument would require studying Hawking's paper. The moderator, a respected professor from the University of London, John G. Taylor, closed the session with the words, 'Sorry, Stephen, but this is absolute rubbish.'

In March 1974, Hawking published his discovery of Hawking radiation in the prestigious science magazine *Nature* – still putting a question mark after the title.

Hawking's friend Martin Rees (shown here in 1975), was one of the first to learn of Hawking's discovery of Hawking radiation. Lord Rees later became Astronomer Royal.

A significant breakthrough

Hawking soon published his 'rubbish', in the science magazine *Nature*. Within a few days physicists all over the world were discussing his idea, some calling it the most significant in theoretical physics in years. Penrose later wrote that, 'Hawking's research in classical general relativity was the best anywhere in the world at that time'. Now he had invaded another realm, quantum mechanics, and made a significant breakthrough. His was the first serious, successful attempt to unify the two great theories of the 20th century: Einstein's relativity (the theory that describes gravity at the level of the very large), and quantum mechanics, which involves the very small – molecules, atoms, and elementary particles. Hawking had also shown a willingness to concede he had been wrong. The area of the event horizon of a black hole *can* decrease.

BLACK HOLE EXPLOSIONS?

After discovering Hawking radiation, Hawking suggested the existence of 'primordial black holes' formed not from the collapse of stars but from pressures in the very early universe that could press matter together extremely tightly. As a little black hole became smaller and smaller (due to Hawking radiation), its temperature and rate of emission would increase. The lower the mass, the higher the temperature. Hawking thought that after billions of years, a primordial black hole's eventual disappearance in an explosion (like millions of hydrogen bombs) might be observable in our own time. Such explosions have not been observed.

Simulation of a giant black hole, showing the dramatic turbulence in its accretion disk and the increasing heat of material spiralling nearer and nearer the event horizon.

Going International

In 1973, Hawking, with George Ellis, published his first book, *The Large Scale Structure of Space-Time*. In 1974 he was elected a Fellow of the Royal Society. When invited to spend the next academic year as Sherman Fairchild Distinguished Scholar at the California Institute of Technology, he accepted.

Stephen and Jane Hawking began a practice of asking a graduate or post-doctoral research student to live and travel with them, receiving free accommodation and extra academic attention in return for helping Hawking get to bed and get up. The first 'graduate assistant', Bernard Carr, accompanied them to California, as did several of Hawking's PhD students, merging temporarily there with physicist Kip Thorne's Cal Tech research group. In his introduction to Hawking's final book, *Brief Answers to the Big Questions*, 2018, Thorne described this year, 1974–75, as 'a glorious year ... at the pinnacle of what came to be called "the golden age of black hole research".' Hawking began the habit of returning to California almost every year.

The information paradox

During his first visit in California, Hawking began pondering a problem later dubbed the 'information paradox' (see also p. 31): what happens to information about everything that becomes part of a black hole when it forms, and everything that falls in later. If a black hole gets smaller and eventually disappears entirely, does all this information vanish from the universe? According to the long-respected law of 'information conservation', information is never lost. If it were, science would lose its ability to predict anything. We would lose our ability to rely on cause and effect. Hawking was still trying to resolve this problem at the time of his death.

In 1974–75, Hawking and his family spent a landmark year at the California Institute of Technology. He was Sherman Fairchild Distinguished Scholar.

Hawking paid working visits to colleagues at other American universities. Here, photographed in October 1979, he was at Princeton University in New Jersey.

Lucasian Professor

Even before that sabbatical in California, Hawking had found that pulling himself up a staircase by the strength of his arms alone was becoming impossible. Upon his return, Gonville and Caius College provided a house that could accommodate a wheelchair, with no stairs. Hawking had completed his six-year Caius Fellowship for Distinction in Science. He could not lecture, but was a fine mentor, devoting so much time to students that colleagues marvelled at his getting his own work done. In 1976, the Royal Society awarded him the Hughes Medal for 'an original discovery in the physical sciences' for 'distinguished contributions to the application of general relativity to astrophysics' and 'for revolutionizing international scientific thought on cosmic black holes'.

In 1977 the University promoted Hawking to a professorship, and in 1978 he won the most prestigious American award for a physicist, the Albert Einstein Award. In 1979, Cambridge appointed him Lucasian Professor of Mathematics, the position (once held by Isaac Newton) that he would occupy for thirty years. When the book where all new university teaching officers inscribed their names was brought to him, he with great difficulty signed his name for the last time. The same year, 1979, saw the birth of the Hawking's third child, Tim.

In 1978 Hawking was honoured with the most prestigious American award for a physicist, the Albert Einstein Award.

No Boundary!

Revisiting the birth of the universe

Early in his career Hawking, like most mathematicians, had been satisfied only with firm mathematical proof that he was correct. By 1980 his attitude had changed. He told Kip Thorne, 'I would rather be right than rigorous'. Mathematical rigour was not, he decided, necessarily the only way to arrive at 'right'. He would allow himself to become more speculative – perhaps 95 percent sure, but then moving on.

When the 1980s began, Hawking could still speak with his own voice, but only those who knew him best could understand him. His graduate assistant delivered his lectures, with Hawking adding brief comments.

After his year-long visit to California Institute of Technology in 1974–75, Hawking returned there almost every year to work with faculty and students. This photo was taken in 1983.

In the summer of 1982, Hawking was working with physicist Jim Hartle at the University of California's new Institute of Theoretical Physics. With Hartle, he turned once more to the question of how the universe began, this time adopting his new preference for thinking more speculatively. He and Hartle called their new idea the 'no-boundary *proposal*', rather than a discovery or theory. That proposal would be seen by many as removing the need for a Creator. Paradoxically, it would incorporate a view of time reminiscent of the ancient Judeo-Christian concept (from the Jewish philosopher Philo of Alexandria and the Christian theologian, St Augustine) of a God existing outside time – the 'I Am' of the Bible – for whom beginnings, endings or anything like chronological time do not exist. That way of looking at time was not new to philosophy or religion, but it was to physics.

The Centre for Mathematical Sciences in Cambridge, where Hawking had his office in the twenty-first century, in the 'pod' visible in the distance on the left.

Four dimensional space

Hawking summed up the no-boundary proposal in this way: 'in the very early universe, when space was very compressed, the "smearing effect" of the uncertainty principle (see p. 17) could change the basic distinction between space and time – and it is then more accurate to talk, not of spacetime, but of *four-dimensional space*.'

If the time dimension becomes a fourth space dimension, asking what happened *before* that, or whether there was a singularity or a Creator before that, or any sort of *boundary* or *beginning* to the universe, becomes as meaningless as asking what is south of the South Pole of the Earth.

In his book, *A Brief History of Time: From the Big Bang to Black Holes*, Hawking later tried to explain this to those without a physics background. 'No boundary' would become a favourite phrase; he was fond of repeating that there should be 'no boundary to human endeavour'.

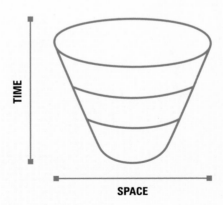

Moving backwards in time towards the beginning of the universe (at the bottom of the diagram), we see the universe contracting in size. At the bottom of the drawing, there is no point of singularity as there was in the drawing on p. 12. Instead, the time dimension changes to a space dimension (horizontal on the diagram).

'Better Off Than I Was Before'

In 1985, Hawking was scheduled to spend a month in Geneva at CERN (Europe's centre for nuclear research). While there, he contracted pneumonia. His wife Jane arrived to find him on life-support, in an induced coma. Doctors gave her the heartbreaking choice: should they perform a tracheotomy to try to save his life; or disconnect the life support and allow him to die? After a tracheotomy, he would never again be able to make any vocal sound. Although his speech was slow and difficult to understand, it was still speech. Without it, what would survival be worth? He could not continue his career or even converse.

For Jane, ending his life was unthinkable. An air ambulance flew him back to Cambridge for the tracheotomy. Recovering slowly, Hawking

After *A Brief History of Time* became a worldwide bestseller in the mid-1980s, Hawking's life changed from that of a highly regarded academic to a global celebrity.

no longer breathed through mouth and nose but through a small opening in his throat near the height of his shirt collar. He could communicate only by spelling out words letter by letter, raising his eyebrows when someone pointed to the right letter on a spelling card.

Unexpectedly, the crisis eventually improved Hawking's ability to communicate. He later insisted, 'I was better off than I was before'. His speech had deteriorated so badly by the time he went to Geneva that even those who knew him well had difficulty understanding him. A 'translator' was required for anyone else. When it seemed that Hawking had completed a sentence, the 'translation' might reveal that he had said only one word. In this painfully slow fashion Hawking had been dictating his academic papers and the first drafts of *A Brief History of Time*. After his surgery and a short hopeless period when it seemed his academic life was over, new technology and wonderful friends came to his rescue.

Back in touch with the world

Kip Thorne and particle physicist Murray Gell-Mann helped Jane Hawking arrange funding for nursing care from the John D. and Catherine T. MacArthur Foundation. A California computer expert,

Walt Woltosz, sent a program written for his disabled mother-in-law. The program, called 'Equalizer' allowed Hawking to select words from a computer screen and had a built-in speech synthesizer. David Mason, the husband of one of Hawking's nurses, adapted a small computer and speech synthesizer to mount on Hawking's wheelchair. He could take his voice with him wherever he went. One of his students rigged up a device like a computer mouse that allowed Hawking to operate the program by a tiny movement still possible for him: squeezing a switch held in his hand. One of his first messages was to his graduate assistant, Brian Whitt, asking Whitt to help him complete *A Brief History of Time*. Soon Hawking could produce ten words a minute. Later his speed improved to more than fifteen. That was not fast, but . . . 'I think slowly', he said.

Hawking in his office at the Cambridge Centre for Mathematical Sciences. He continued 'going into work' (as he referred to it) as often as possible until just weeks before his death.

The Voice System

Equalizer, Hawking's speech program, worked in basically the same way for twenty-five years, before being improved by a more up-to-date system in the 1990s and replaced in the 2010s. A vocabulary of about 2,500 words was programmed into the computer. About 200 were specialized scientific terms.

How Equalizer worked

The screen's top half and bottom half were highlighted alternately, back and forth. When the highlighted half-screen included the word he wanted, Hawking squeezed the switch in his hand to choose that half-screen. Then lines of words on that half-screen were highlighted one after the other. When a highlighted line included the word he wanted, he squeezed the switch again. The words on that line were then highlighted one after the other. When the word he required was highlighted, he pressed the switch again. It worked very rapidly, at the speed of a video game. Sometimes he missed and the whole sequence had to be repeated. There were a few frequently-used phrases: 'Please turn the page', 'Please switch on the desk computer', plus an alphabet for spelling words not included in the program.

Hawking's selected words appeared, one at a time, to make a sentence which appeared across the lower part of the screen. He could then choose, if he wished, to send the sentence to the speech synthesizer that pronounced it out loud or over the telephone. He had a formatting program for writing papers, and he wrote out his equations in words that the program translated into symbols.

Hawking's communication system required him to choose his words one by one from a computer screen, using a small movement of one hand or, when he could no longer manage that, a squint of his cheek muscle.

Public speaking

Hawking composed lectures in this way and saved them on disks. He could print out or rework them and listen in advance to the speech synthesizer delivering the lecture, then continue to edit and polish. In front of an audience, he sent the lecture to the speech synthesizer a sentence at a time. An assistant showed slides, wrote Hawking's equations on the board, and answered some questions.

Hawking insisted that technology developed for him be made available to others. Here, he is still able to trigger his system with a faint pressure from his hand.

Open source

In the 2000s, improvements from the tech company Intel enabled Hawking to use his speech system and the internet more efficiently. An Intel team and his student 'technical assistants' struggled to keep him communicating when the muscles he required (first in his hand and later his facial muscles) inevitably failed him. The Intel team and he would never give up, even in the weeks before his death. Hawking had insisted that everything Intel developed to help him communicate be made 'open source' and available to anyone else who needed it.

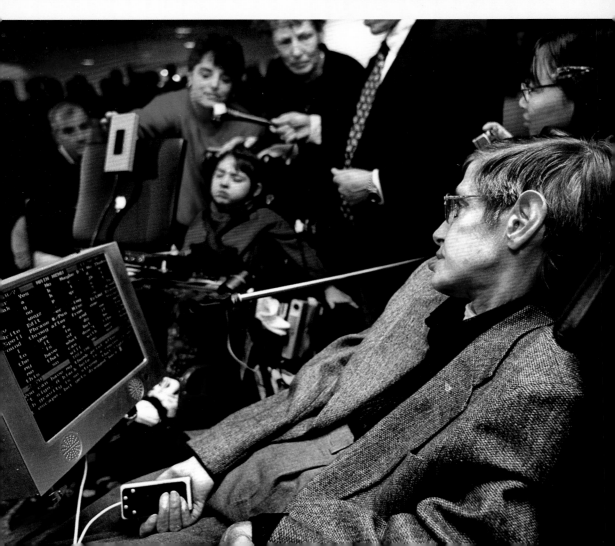

International Honours

By autumn 1986, Hawking was fully involved in physics again. He was appointed to the Pontifical Academy of Sciences and awarded the Institute of Physics's first Paul Dirac Medal. In 1988 he won the Wolf Prize, awarded by the Wolf Foundation of Israel and recognized as second in prestige only to a Nobel Prize. In 1989, the Queen named him a Companion of Honour.

The price of fame

In the late 1980s, *A Brief History of Time* reached bestseller lists all over the world. Stephen Hawking was now not only a highly respected scholar but also an international celebrity, and he loved the spotlight and media hype. Unfortunately, his wife and family did not. In 1990, Hawking took responsibility publicly for the rupture when he left Jane for one of his nurses, Elaine Mason. Until Jane published her book *Music to Move the Stars*, ten years later, no one outside close friends and family was aware of how troubled the Hawkings' marriage had been, or of her long, intimate relationship with choir master Jonathan Hellyer Jones. Hawking and Elaine Mason married in 1995 and divorced eleven years later, in 2006. Jane and Jonathan Hellyer Jones married in 1997.

How many universes?

While Hawking radiation and the no-boundary proposal are considered Hawking's most significant contributions, he was also involved in the development of theories initiated by others. From the late 1970s, when physicists Alan Guth and Andrei Linde proposed that the universe, early-on, had undergone a brief interval of stupendously rapid expansion, Hawking became interested in the development of 'inflation theory'. He contributed important papers about 'eternal inflation' after Linde and Alex Vilenkin suggested that an inflationary universe can 'self- reproduce', resulting in an enormous fractal arrangement of universes sprouting one out of another. In this theory, our universe is one of perhaps an infinite number of universes in the 'multiverse'.

Hawking with the wax figure of himself at Madame Tussauds. He enjoyed being a celebrity.

Hawking and his first wife Jane in the late 1980s.

This suggestion seemed to answer a question that Hawking had long been asking: why is our universe so inexplicably fine-tuned to allow life like ours to exist? In an infinite number of universes, there is almost sure to be one like ours.

Gravitational waves and supertranslation

Hawking was central to discussion following the observation in September 2015 of gravitational waves emanating from the collision of two black holes 1.3 billion light years away. He also continued to work on the information paradox. At the time of his death he and colleagues were addressing that problem in a promising way, with 'supertranslations theory', in which what seems irrevocably lost in a black hole is preserved in holographic form at the event horizon. Hawking's last paper on this subject, with Sasha Haco, Malcolm Perry and Andrew Strominger, was published after his death, in the autumn of 2018.

A final about-face

A paper with physicist Thomas Hertog, completed just days before Hawking died, proposed that the very early universe could be described by a theory with just three spatial dimensions and no fourth dimension at all! The physics in such a situation did not necessarily lead to eternal inflation and an infinite number of universes. It might end up with a single, unique universe – ours.

Hawking and Elaine Mason were wed in 1995.

Using Celebrity

In his last two decades Hawking used his celebrity and intellectual prestige to support causes he felt were vitally important. He favoured listening for evidence of extraterrestrial life but warned against trying to make contact. He urged that the development of artificial intelligence be carefully controlled. He spoke out on political issues, and particularly on behalf of disabled people, encouraging them by what he said and by his powerful example. He led the brilliant opening ceremony of the 2012 London Paralympic Games. He forecast an apocalyptic future for the Earth, urging humans to find ways to colonize other planets.

On a lighter note, Hawking played himself in *Star Trek: The Next Generation* – 'Descent' (Part One), first screened in 1993; in *The Simpsons*, in ten episodes beginning in 1999 with 'They Saved Lisa's Brain'; and in *The Big Bang Theory*, in seven episodes beginning in 2012 with 'The Hawking Excitation'.

Closer to home, Hawking enjoyed visits from his grandchildren and threw parties with spectacular firework displays for family and friends. After all the terrifying physical crises, the failure of two marriages, dire warnings about Earth's future, and inexorable erosion of his ability to communicate, he remained to the end the intensely curious child he had been in the fields at Osmington Mills, eager for adventure, insisting that the work he did was fun and wanting everyone to share that fun. The famous grin never failed.

He died on 14 March 2018. At his funeral in Cambridge, and at Westminster Abbey when his ashes were interred, crowds thronged the streets, paying tribute to a life well lived.

Hawking took a zero-gravity flight in 2007 and proudly posted this photo on his office door.